sixths for the cello

book one

by cassia harvey

CHP141

©2005 by C. Harvey Publications All Rights Reserved.

www.charveypublications.com - print books
www.learnstrings.com - PDF downloadable books
www.harveystringarrangements.com - chamber music

Part One: C Major

1

C to D

Cassia Harvey

Shift a whole step on the top & half step on the bottom.

Shift; don't stretch.

Canon

Tallis, arr. C. Harvey

©2005 C. Harvey Publications All Rights Reserved.

C to D to E to F

Menuet
Exaudet, arr. C. Harvey

F to G

Shift a whole step on the top & whole step on the bottom.

Ode to Joy

Beethoven, arr. C. Harvey

8 E to G

Symphony Theme — Dvorak, arr. C. Harvey

11 — B to C

Minuet
Corrette, arr. C. Harvey

12   G to C

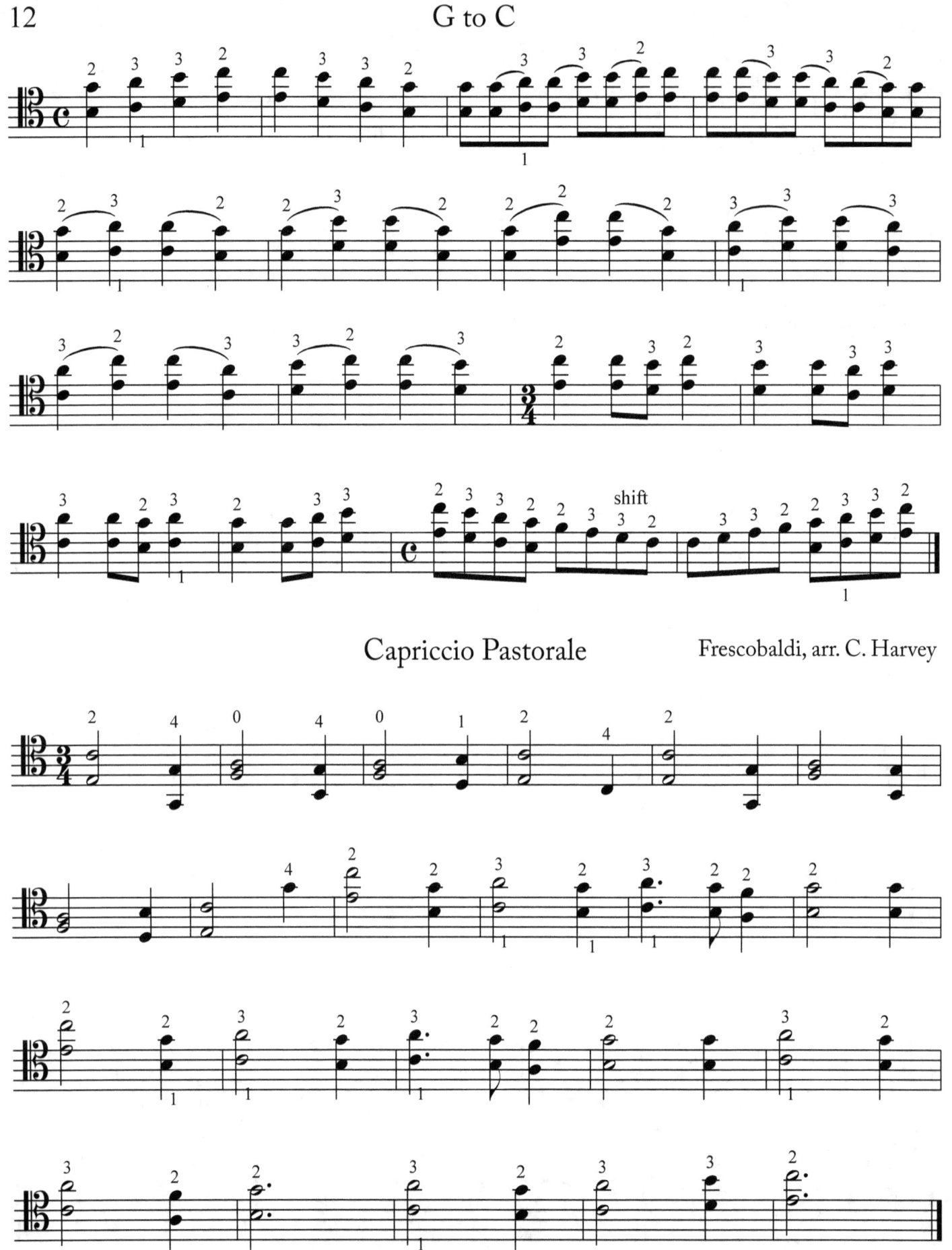

Capriccio Pastorale   Frescobaldi, arr. C. Harvey

13

C major scale

Allegretto

Cramer, arr. C. Harvey

Sixths for the Cello, Book One

Part Two: B♭ Major   B♭ to E♭
16

Use the correct fingerings here:
3-1 for a whole step space, 2-1 for a half step space.

Simple Gifts
Traditional, arr. C. Harvey

16   ©2005 C. Harvey Publications All Rights Reserved.

Sixths for the Cello, Book One

18. E♭ through A

Use the correct fingerings here.

Johnston Gals
Traditional, arr. C. Harvey

19 F through B♭

Use the correct fingerings here.

Mary Hamilton Traditional, arr. C. Harvey

Part Three: D major

21
D to G

Hartigan's Fancy
Traditional, arr. C. Harvey

22

F♯ to B

Mairi's Wedding
Traditional, arr. C. Harvey

24 D major scale

Vivace

Haydn, arr. C. Harvey

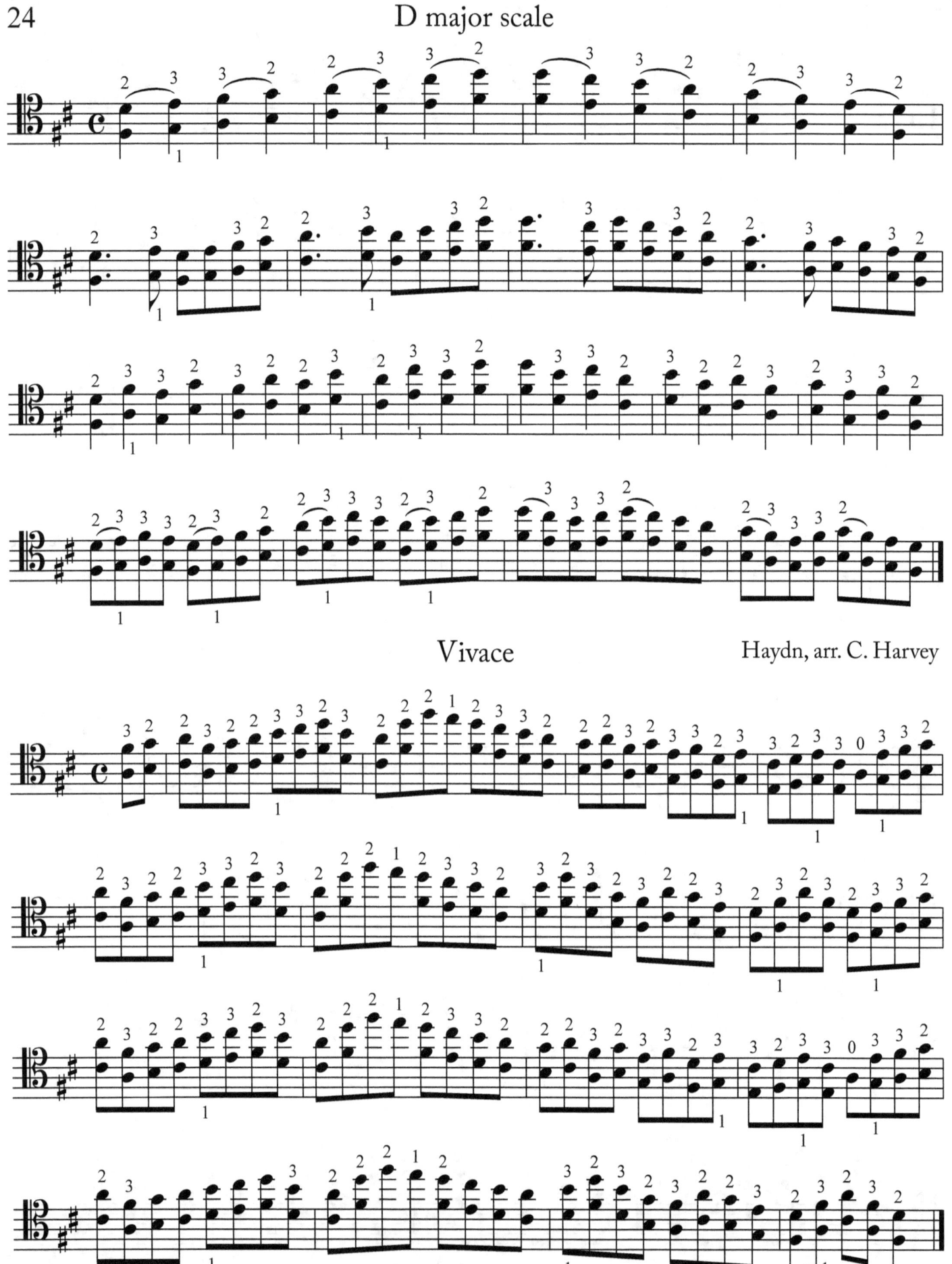

Part Four: E♭ Major

25

E♭ to A♭

St. Anthony's Chorale

Haydn, arr. C. Harvey

26

G to C

Polovtsian Dances

Borodin, arr. C. Harvey

Sixths for the Cello, Book One

28
E♭ major scale

Gavotte
Handel, arr. C. Harvey

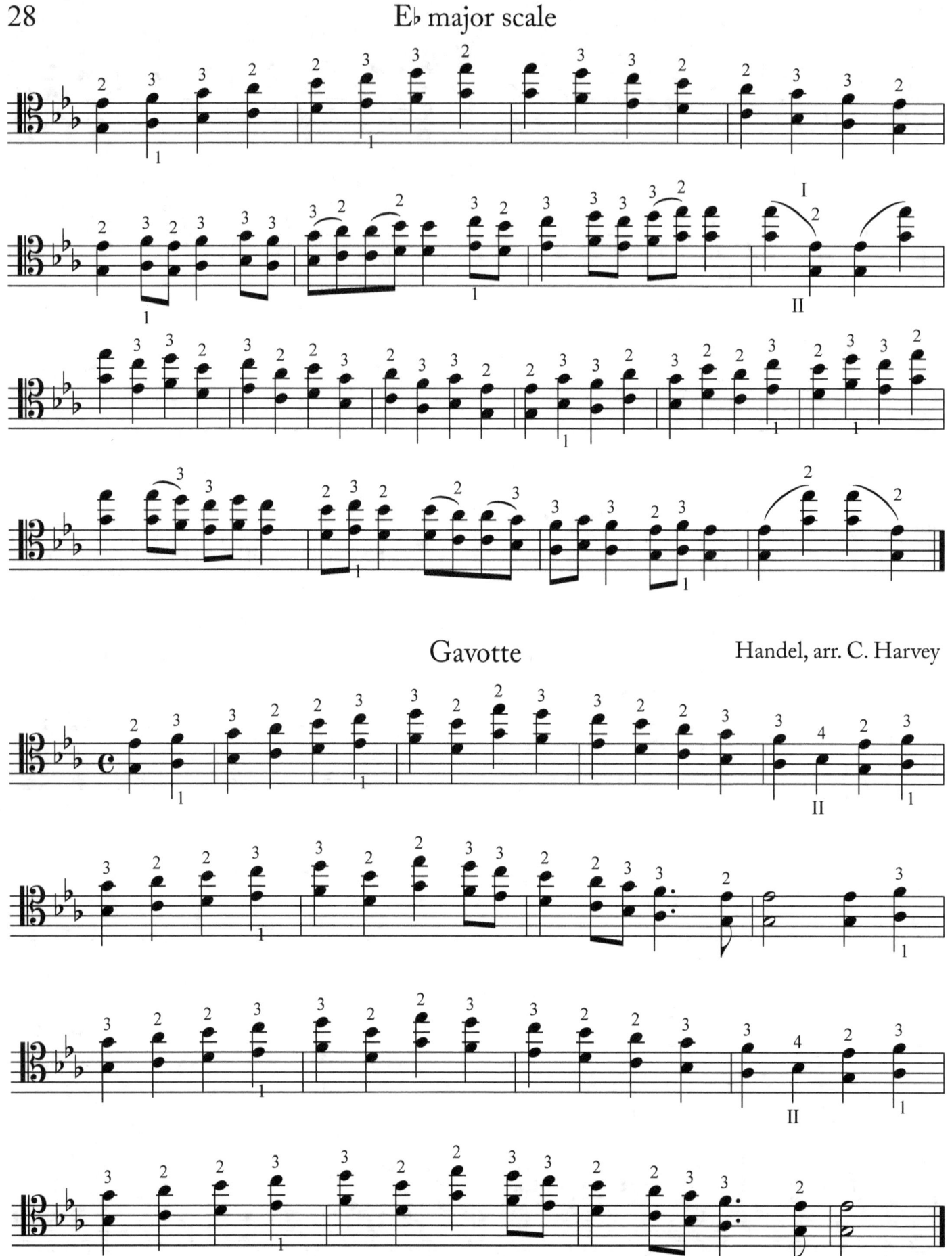

©2005 C. Harvey Publications All Rights Reserved.

Part Five: Other Scales

29
B major scale

Study
Lee, arr. C. Harvey

30

D♭ major scale

The Girl I Left Behind Me
Traditional, arr. C. Harvey

32 F major scale

Theme from Horn Concerto #1
Mozart, arr. C. Harvey

Also available from www.charveypublications.com: CHP349
The Saint-Saens Cello Concerto No. 1 Study Book, Vol. 1

www.ingramcontent.com/pod-product-compliance
Lightning Source LLC
Chambersburg PA
CBHW051429070526
44584CB00023B/3642